SHE'S NOBODY'S BABY
A HISTORY OF AMERICAN WOMEN IN THE 20TH CENTURY

EDITED BY SUZANNE BRAUN LEVINE
WRITTEN BY SUSAN DWORKIN

INTRODUCED BY ALAN ALDA AND
MARLO THOMAS

PHOTO RESEARCH: SHEREE CRUTE

DESIGN: STEVE PHILLIPS
AND LESLIE MORRIS

A FIRESIDE BOOK
PUBLISHED BY SIMON & SCHUSTER, INC.
NEW YORK

Simon & Schuster Building
Rockefeller Center
1230 Avenue of the Americas
New York, New York 10020

FIRESIDE and colophon are registered
trademarks of Simon & Schuster, Inc.

Designed by Steve Phillips and Leslie Morris
Typesetting by Nancy Fried Zankel

Manufactured in the United States of America

2 3 4 5 6 7 8 9 10

ISBN: 0-671-49247-0

SHE'S NOBODY'S BABY
A HISTORY OF AMERICAN WOMEN IN THE 20TH CENTURY

QUESTIONS AND ANSWERS
BY MARLO THOMAS

What we call "The Women's Movement" has been an effort on the part of roughly one hundred million Americans not to be trivialized or patronized or fantasized about any more—but to be treated as equal individuals, protected by reality, protected by law and one day soon by the Constitution. We began by wrestling with the fantasies we seemed to be born into—and to consider whether or not they were actually true.

Was it actually true that women were better off being weak and dependent? Was it actually true that men liked supporting everybody all by themselves? Was it unfeminine to want power:

disfiguring to stand out in a crowd? Were career women really abrasive and housewives really nothing much at all?

It was a very long question-and-answer period. And it brought women of every race and political persuasion, every income level and religion, into rooms and little restaurants together, privately, just talking.

We talked to our mothers and learned for the first time what they were so angry about.

We talked to the funny-looking ones, who said they felt imprisoned by their bodies, and the pretty ones, who said they felt imprisoned by their bodies. We learned that as long as women were defined by what they looked like—funny-looking; pretty—their bodies would be political prisons, where of course, their rights were irrelevant.

We began to see that we had a struggle in common.

What had begun as a night out with the girls was turning out to be its own kind of Bund meeting.

As we began to understand each other, we dried the tears and said to each other: "Sister, I am on your side. We are in this together."

In this way, the biggest civil rights movement ever mounted in any country was born.

There is no American it has not touched.

REMEMBER SENECA FALLS
BY ALAN ALDA

Without the events of Seneca Falls, the story of "She's Nobody's Baby" would be very different.

It was there, half a century before our story begins, in 1848, that Lucretia Mott and Elizabeth Cady Stanton called the convention that began the fight for suffrage. It was there in 1923 that Alice Paul first introduced the Equal Rights Amendment. And in 1982, the simple, stark rooms where the early feminists met and strategized were dedicated as the National Women's Rights Historical Park.

In keeping with the continuing commitment to full equality for women, people are already mobilizing for another ground-breaking event to be associated with Seneca Falls: the formation of a National Women's Center, which would coordinate feminist research, information, fund raising, networking, and generally help harness the momentum of women's political, social, and economic emergence. Given the energy and courage that Seneca Falls already stands for, this too should come to pass.

The essay that follows is adapted from a speech Alan Alda gave at the Dedication of the Women's Rights National Park on July 17, 1982.

Exactly 134 years ago Elizabeth Cady Stanton walked the streets of Seneca Falls with these words in her head: "We hold these truths to be self evident—that all men and women are created equal." And when she presented that Declaration of Sentiments at the Women's Rights Convention on July 20, 1848, she drew not only on the historic words of Thomas Jefferson, but on the cry for freedom that had animated the American Revolution—"No taxation without representation." She asked for something that was, at the time, almost unheard of—the right for women to vote.

We need to remember.

The courage of that act is almost unimaginable today. We take it for granted that women should have the right to vote.

Without the memory of the people who have gone before us, we are constantly forced to start from scratch each time we try to move forward. The day is past when the history of women can be written in invisible ink.

America's forefathers had the heroes of antiquity to look back to. Not only Jefferson and Adams, but all the educated people of their time had Greek and Roman philosophers, statesmen, and generals to draw on.

How many educated people today know much of anything at all about Stanton, Anthony, Wollstonecraft, Fuller, Stone, Mott, Chapman Catt, Amelia Bloomer, or Sojourner Truth?

We need these women's guidance, their wisdom, their example—we need the power of their lives. By writing strong women out of history, we've left ourselves only with an image of women as inoffensive sweetness.

We are trying to run a car on a tank filled half with fuel and half with sugar.

We need to remember Abigail Adams who said in 1776 to her husband John: "Whilst you are proclaiming peace and good will to men, emancipating all nations, you insist upon retaining an absolute power over wives."

And Margaret Fuller who in 1845 said: "Inward and outward, freedom for woman as much as for man shall be acknowledged as a *right*, not yielded as a concession... Man cannot, by right, lay even well meant restrictions on woman."

And Lucy Stone, who said in 1881: "The widening of woman's sphere is to improve her lot. Let us do it, and if the world scoff, let it scoff—if it sneer, let it sneer... We want rights."

And Susan B. Anthony, who said in 1868: "Men, their rights and nothing more; women, their rights and nothing less."

With their strong voices in our ears, I believe that recent defeats notwithstanding, America will finally declare one day that "equality of rights under the law shall not be denied or abridged by the United States or by any State on account of sex."

We cannot settle for half a measure of freedom.

Too many women have devoted their lives to equality. Too many women have died without seeing it come to pass.

Elizabeth Cady Stanton drew on Jefferson, let us look to Seneca Falls and draw on Lincoln.

"Six score and fourteen years ago, our mothers brought forth on this continent a new notion—conceived in liberty and dedicated to the proposition that all men and women are created equal.

"Now we are engaged in a great struggle, testing whether that notion or any notion so conceived and so dedicated can long endure. We are met in a town that gave birth to struggle. We have come to dedicate a portion of this town as a shrine to those who here devoted their lives that this notion might live. It is altogether fitting and proper that we should do this.

"But, in a larger sense, we cannot dedicate, we cannot consecrate, we cannot hallow this ground. The brave women, living and dead, who struggle here have consecrated it far above our poor power to add or detract.

"The world will little note nor long remember what we say here, but it can never forget what they did here. It is for us, the living, rather to be dedicated here to the unfinished work which they, who fought here, have thus far so nobly advanced.

"It is rather for us to be here dedicated to the great task remaining before us—that from these honored women we take increased devotion to that cause for which they gave the last full measure of devotion—that we here highly resolve that these women shall not have lived and died in vain, that this nation under God shall have a new birth of freedom and that government of the people, by the people, for the people shall not perish from the earth."

SHE'S NOBODY'S BABY
A HISTORY OF AMERICAN WOMEN IN THE 20TH CENTURY

SHE'S NOBODY'S BABY

No one...but no one...has received more advice during the last eighty years than the average American woman. How to dress; whom to marry; when to cry. What was healthy; what was evil; what to buy. She was supposed to be what the times demanded. The 1900s, for example, demanded innocence. In 1908, the *Ladies Home Journal* gave her this advice on sex: Holding a boy's hand before marriage, said the *Journal,* can lead to "crippling illness and disease!"

The 1960s, however, asked her to be someone quite different. Books like Helen Gurley Brown's *Sex and the Office* were giving her advice on how to conduct an affair on her lunch hour. (The thing she had to watch was her hair. If she came back to the office with "locks of damp hair" from the post-passion shower, everyone in the typing pool was going to know she wasn't having lunch at lunch.)

And so it went, from generation to generation. Conflicting advice...from the government, the clergy...from the doctors, the bosses...from the media, the mothers, the fathers, the lovers; they all told the American woman: do this, do that. Was it any wonder that she was finally fed up with advice?

But the seventies became her times. At last, she demanded to be treated like a grown-up. She began to pick and choose which advice she would—and would not—listen to. And now...She's nobody's baby.

DATES FROM THE DECADE

1910

National Association for the Advancement of Colored People founded.

1912

New Mexico and Arizona become the last mainland states to join the union.

Titanic sinks.

Discovery of vitamins by Casimir Funk.

Woodrow Wilson elected President.

1913

Harriet Tubman, heroine of the Underground Railroad, dies a pauper.

1914

Panama Canal opens.

1915

Transcontinental telephone service inaugurated.

1917

Jeannette Rankin of Montana becomes the first woman in Congress.

Congress declares war on Germany.

1918

President Wilson announces his "14 Points" for peace.
Armistice signed.

1919

18th Amendment (Prohibition) ratified.

The turn of the century appeared to be rather placid. Romantic.

Hats were large. And flowery. And feathery. Skirts were long. Very long. Only tables dared to show their legs.

Every woman was supposed to be somebody's baby.

The fashion dream girl of the times strapped herself up in a corset and crinolines. She went in at the middle, out in the front, and tried to look as much as possible like an S. No wonder women were considered so delicate; with all that choking pressure on lungs and abdomen, they were often on the verge of passing out from S-ness.

Alice Roosevelt

But the President's daughter, Alice Roosevelt, epitomized a new spirit. In *one year* she attended 402 dances. She was the prototype for Charles Dana Gibson's haughty, independent "Gibson Girl," who got rid of the yards of bustles and ruffles encumbering her stride and adopted a tailored skirt she could actually *move* in. Theodore Roosevelt found it easier to be President than Alice's father.

"I can run the country, or I can control Alice, but I can't do both!"

—Theodore Roosevelt

I Don't Care

Alice as a youngster with her family and her hat

A popular song of the day

DANGER!

ALL SHE ASKED.

HE (at the soirée): May I not offer you some refreshment?
"Yes. Just give me a few minutes to myself."

DELAYS ARE DANGEROUS

"Now, my dear, you ought to go right into housekeeping as soon as you are married."
"That is the best time to begin, I suppose, while I am sure of George's love."

G ood girls were innocent—a nice way of saying ignorant. On the screen we had Mary Pickford. And Lillian Gish; her costume was virginity; her promise was love.

The bad girl was the vamp.

Her costume was scanty. Her promise was sex.

The top vamp, Theda Bara, seemed so evil that she *had* to be foreign. In truth, she was Theodosia Goodman from Chicago. But her screen name was an anagram of Arab Death.

Actress Pola Negri went Bara one better. She smoked.

But most American women weren't virgins or vamps. Most were just working.

Theda Bara

Pola Negri

19

By 1910, fifty-five percent of black women and twenty-three percent of all women worked for wages.

The housewife could usually look forward to an 18-hour day of non-stop drudgery. Doing laundry by hand without hot running water. Scrubbing wooden floors. Baking bread before breakfast. The farm woman did all that and worked beside her man in the fields too. The factory woman went home after work, and worked some more.

The industrial system employed children as young as six and seven in mines and canneries and airless mills. Playing in the sunshine quickly became a distant memory.

A nd then there were the immigrants. By 1910, they made up half the population of every major American city. Since the turn of the century 8,795,386 immigrants had arrived. The total U.S. population reached 91,972,000.

They arrived with great hopes, often to find their dreams—and their names—changed against their will. They were expecting a golden land. They landed in the worst slums America had ever seen.

Medical exam at Ellis Island

Tenement family

V ery often, an immigrant woman did piecework to supplement her family's income. Every day she delivered it back to the factory and picked up some more. If she worked as hard as she could, she might earn an extra thirty-five cents a day at a time when one loaf of bread cost five cents.

The average earnings of a male immigrant were $566 a year; a woman made $307; a child could earn $186 and in rural areas $158.

One wife whose doctor said she would *die* with another pregnancy asked him for advice on that most taboo of subjects—birth control. He had none: "Tell Jake to sleep on the roof," he said.

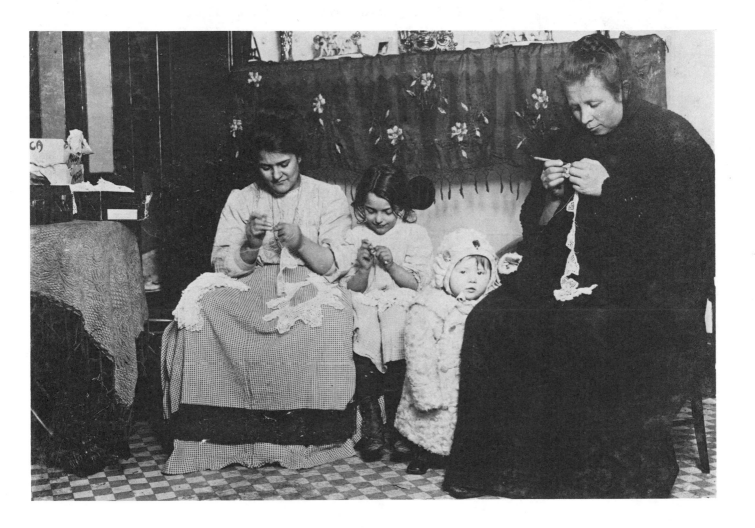

Often the only jobs available to urban slum women were in sweatshops where they worked long hours, straining their eyes and backs and pushing themselves to meet harsh quotas. Often they had to bring their own sewing machines and buy needles and thread from their employers.

Mamma nursed the baby and ate at the same time. She ate mechanically, too tired to taste the food. Between mouthfuls she kissed the baby's head. When the baby was satisfied, she was too, and handed the boy the baby and the pot. Then, without looking at them again, she went back to work, pedaling like mad.
—From *Bride of the Sabbath* by Samuel Ornitz

In March 1911, fire broke out at the Triangle Shirtwaist Factory in New York.

The doors had been locked—to keep the girls from going to the bathroom and to keep organizers of the infant American labor movement from getting in. Six men and 140 young Jewish and Italian working women were killed. Some jumped. Some burned.

Even relatives had trouble identifying the dead.

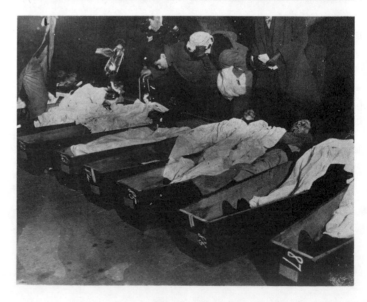

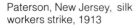

Rosie Schneiderman at
union rally

The Triangle fire galvanized efforts to create trade unions among the garment workers. And in the forefront of that movement was Rosie Schneiderman. "I would be a traitor to these poor burned bodies," she said, "if I came here to talk of good fellowship. It is up to working people to save themselves."

Schneiderman was one of an unprecedented generation of women reformers who couldn't remain "placid" in the face of overwhelming need.

Paterson, New Jersey, silk
workers strike, 1913

Women like Lillian Wald, whose visiting nurses worked in neighborhoods where male physicians rarely ventured. Later, she persuaded the Board of Education to put nurses into the schools. Her arguments were not about politics, but about "little Louie, the deplorable condition of whose scalp is denying him the blessing of education."

Women like Florence Kelley, who was horrified "by the utter unimportance of children compared with products in the minds of the people...." She fought to abolish child labor, and she won.

Women like Jane Addams, who realized that private charity was "totally inadequate to deal with the vast numbers of the city's disinherited." She started settlement houses where poor families could get a hot meal and learn the language.

Florence Kelley

Lillian Wald

Jane Addams

In 1916 more than one hundred nurses often climbed tenement rooftops to make 227,000 visits to the poor.

Mary McLeod Bethune

Women like Mary McLeod Bethune. In 1904 she started a school for black children on the site of an old garbage dump in Daytona, Florida. They sold homemade pies to make ends meet. They slept on mattresses of straw. The school's benefactor was black hair culturist and self-made millionaire Madam C.J. Walker.

"If our people are to fight their way up out of bondage, we must arm them with the sword and the shield and the buckles of *pride*."

—Mary McLeod Bethune

"Mother" Mary Harris Jones on the march

The labor organizer Mother Jones, who led the miners of Colorado out on strike, had a new and unusual advice for women of conscience. "Whatever the fight, don't be ladylike!"

And incredibly, all kinds of women began standing up and speaking out for the social causes *they* believed in, from Temperance to suffrage, from police reform to pacifism.

The First World War was starting, and many suffragists opposed it. How could we fight to defend democracy, they wanted to know, when half the people in *our* democracy couldn't even vote?

The soldiers had gone out like knights on horseback. They came back wounded, wised-up, modern men. By the war's end in 1918, 325,000 Americans had been killed, or captured, or wounded. At home, almost twice as many—over 600,000 *more* Americans—died in the epidemic of Spanish flu. The black and the immigrant poor were hit the hardest. Women nursed them all; saw it all.

**I didn't raise my boy to be a soldier.
I brought him up to be my pride and joy.
Who dared to place a musket on his shoulder,
to kill another mother's darling boy?**

—Written during World War I, this song was banned for being unpatriotic

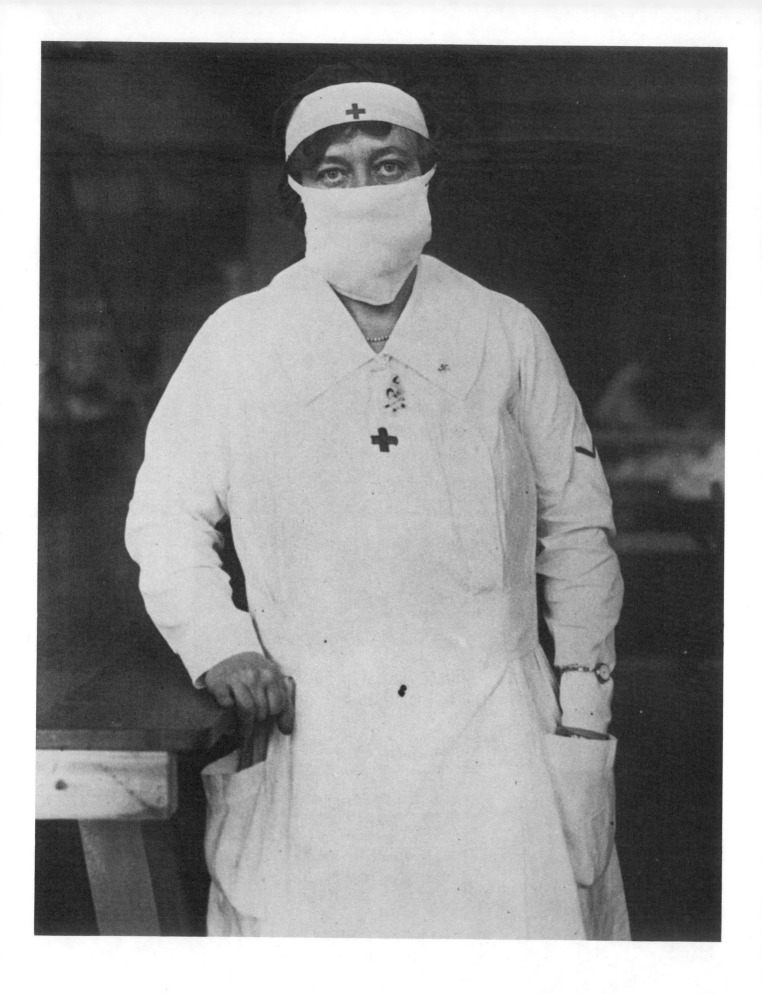

In the wake of the war and the flu, words like "placid" and "romantic" seemed as obsolete as the horses of the old army.

It was the end of innocence, the end of ignorance. The demands of grown-up women could no longer be denied.

Women in frontier territories like Wyoming, Colorado, and Utah had won the vote in the 1800s, but it was 1920 before the Suffrage Amendment was passed.

"This heresy of women's rights [will] lead women to become unsexed and turn gentle mothers into Amazonian brawlers"

—sexologist William Walling, 1904

SUFFRAGETTE SERIES Nº II.

EVERYBODY
WORKS BUT
MOTHER:
SHE'S A
SUFFRAGETT

I WANT TO VOTE, BUT
MY·WIFE·WONT·LET·ME

COPYRIGHTED 1909 BY DUNSTON-WEILER LITHOGRAPH CO.

That "Amazonian brawler," Carrie Chapman Catt, spoke of the long struggle for the vote: "To get that word, 'male,' out of the Constitution, cost the women of this country 52 years of pauseless campaign; 56 state referendum campaigns; 480 legislative campaigns; 277 state party convention campaigns, 30 national party convention campaigns to get suffrage planks in the party platforms; 19 campaigns with 19 successive Congresses to get the federal amendment submitted, and the final ratification campaign....

"Millions of dollars were raised, mostly in small sums, and spent with economic care. Hundreds of women gave the accumulated possibilities of a lifetime, thousands gave years of their lives, hundreds of thousands gave constant interest and such aid as they could. It was a continuous and seemingly endless chain of activity. Young suffragists who helped forge the last links of that chain were not born when it began. Old suffragists who helped forge the first links were dead when it ended."

"It took George Washington six years to rectify men's grievances by war. But it took seventy-two years to establish women's rights by law. Women's suffrage is a long story of hard work and heartache crowned by victory."

—Carrie Chapman Catt

42

DATES FROM THE DECADE

1920
Warren G. Harding elected President.

1921
First Miss America contest held.

1922
King Tut's tomb discovered.

1923
Harding dies; Calvin Coolidge becomes President.

1925
John Scopes convicted for teaching evolution

1926
Gertrude Ederle becomes first woman to swim the English Channel.

1927
The Jazz Singer starring Al Jolson, first talking picture, opens.
Charles A. Lindbergh flies first non-stop solo flight from New York to Paris.

1928
Herbert Hoover elected President.

1929
St. Valentine's Day Massacre, peak of gangster war.

A tango with Rudolph Valentino

All those dough-boys returning from the war in France gave America a new sense of connection to the style and sophistication of Europe. And Europe sent us the tango. Now, an S-shaped woman cannot dance the tango. So, in came the short-line bra, the short–line girdle. Short hair. Short skirts. In short, in came the flapper.

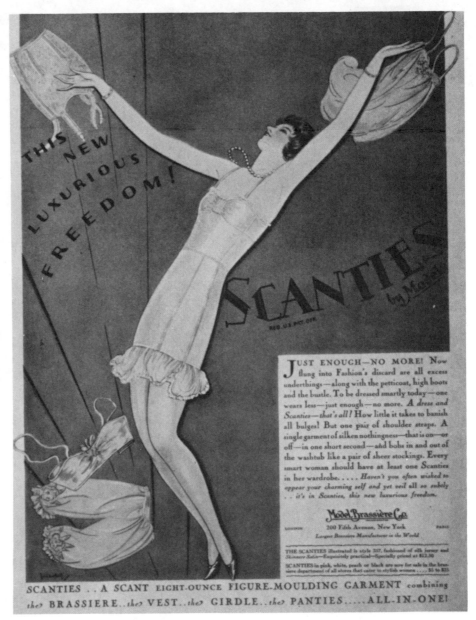

THIS NEW LUXURIOUS FREEDOM!

SCANTIES by Model
REG. U.S. PAT. OFF.

JUST ENOUGH—NO MORE! Now flung into Fashion's discard are all excess underthings—along with the petticoat, high boots and the bustle. To be dressed smartly today—one wears less—just enough—no more. A dress and Scanties—that's all! How little it takes to banish all bulges! But one pair of shoulder straps. A single garment of silken nothingness—that is on—or off—in one short second—and bobs in and out of the washtub like a pair of sheer stockings. Every smart woman should have at least one Scanties in her wardrobe..... Haven't you often wished to appear your charming self and yet veil all so subtly ... it's in Scanties, this new luxurious freedom.

Model Brassiere Co.
LONDON   200 Fifth Avenue, New York   PARIS
Largest Brassiere Manufacturer in the World

THE SCANTIES illustrated is style 357, fashioned of silk jersey and Skinsere Satin—Exquisitely practical—Specially priced at $12.50

SCANTIES in pink, white, peach or black are now for sale in the brassiere department of all stores that cater to stylish women.... $5 to $25

SCANTIES . . A SCANT EIGHT-OUNCE FIGURE-MOULDING GARMENT combining the BRASSIERE..the VEST..the GIRDLE..the PANTIES.....ALL-IN-ONE!

The Charleston

The flapper of the twenties learned to drink precisely when Prohibition had made it illegal. She gave up her long skirt and took up fast dancing. Her ideal was Zelda Fitzgerald, who married author F. Scott Fitzgerald, and spoke for her generation: "... The Flapper awoke from her lethargy of sub-deb-ism, bobbed her hair, put on her choicest pair of earrings and a great deal of audacity and rouge and went into battle. She flirted because it was fun to flirt and wore a one-piece bathing suit because she had a good figure; she covered her face with powder and paint because she didn't need it, and she refused to be bored chiefly because she wasn't boring."

Zelda Fitzgerald

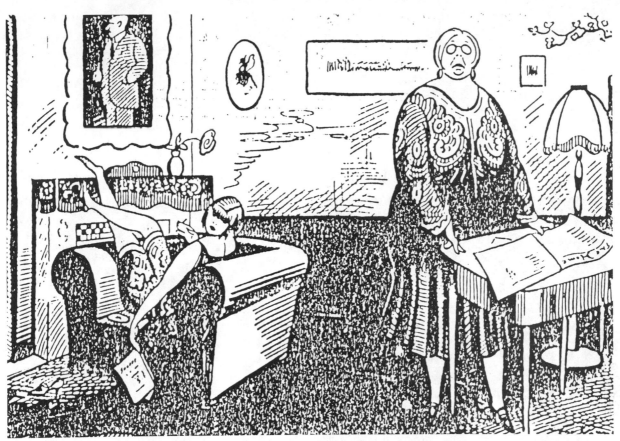

"Mother, when you were a girl, didn't you find it a bore to be a virgin?"

Flapper twins

The IT girl of the movies, Clara Bow was never bored—because she flirted better than anyone.

Fanny Brice

Fanny Brice as Baby Snooks
opposite Judy Garland in
Everybody Sing, 1938

Fanny Brice as Eve opposite
Bobby Clark in *The Music
Box Review*, 1924

And nobody *spoofed* the vamp better than Fanny Brice, Florenz Ziegfeld's greatest star. She insisted on controlling her own material and managed to be funny without exploiting her sexuality or making a fool of women. Said Katharine Hepburn with admiration, "Fanny had a consideration for artistic integrity that I've never encountered elsewhere."

T he country was enjoying a postwar boom. So a woman's new advisors were the businessmen and their inventive allies, the scientific experts. They promised women Better Living Through Gadgetry. A scientific expert named Freud said that sexual repression could ruin her health. A businessman named Ford invented a car where she and her man could be alone. By 1928, condoms were a $250,000,000 business.

The new woman was a city girl—an office girl—and one boss had this advice for her: "I expect from my stenographer the same service I get from the sun, with this exception: The sun often goes on strike—and it is necessary for me to use artifical light. But I pay my stenographer to work six days out of every seven, and I expect her all the while to radiate my office with sunshine and sympathetic interest in all the things *I* am trying to do."

For the woman who worked at home, the businessmen and the scientific experts marketed new gadgets that were supposed to cut down household time and motion. Hot water on tap. Easy-to-wash linoleum floors. In keeping with the scientific approach, child rearing too was revised along the assembly line. Millions of intimidated mothers attempted to follow the regimen prescribed by a Dr. John Watson, the Dr. Spock of the twenties.

**"One. Treat children as though they were young adults.
Two. Never hug them or kiss them.
Three. Never let them sit on your lap.
Four. If you must, kiss them once on the forehead when they say goodnight.
Five. Shake hands with them in the morning."**

—Dr. John Watson

"I wouldn't kiss him dear—it might cause a maladjustment later on."   © The New Yorker

However, the scientific gadgetry that was supposed to revolutionize houswivery remained an isolated advantage of the upper economic classes until many years later. And it was a nurse—Margaret Sanger—who first understood that the only "science" which could really save women was birth control.

Sanger, whose own mother had 11 children and died at 48, advocated the diaphragm, a woman's method. But, in 1916, when she opened a birth control clinic in New York, the police closed it down and carted her off to jail. Undaunted, she went on to convene the first International Conference on Family Planning.

She looked forward to the day "when motherhood becomes the fruit of a deep yearning... not the result of ignorance or accident..." In the twenties, birth control began to take hold among millions of families, but only on certain conditions mandated by the medical establishment. Yes, the housewife could now have her diaphragm... by appointment... by prescription... from her doctor. And in very short order, the male gynecologist became a woman's chief advisor on sex.

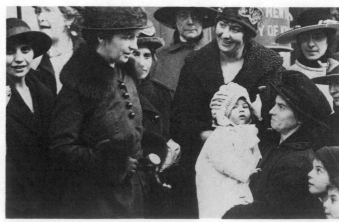

Two out of 100 women actually went to college in the twenties. Business had a formula for their future. If they went to work after school, they were sure to be that greatest of corporate assets—overqualified.

Dr. Edward H. Clark wrote a book called *Sex in Education, or a Fair Chance for the Girls* that proved that higher education would cause women's uteruses to atrophy. President Coolidge called the women's schools "hotbeds of radicalism."

"Women beware. You are on the brink of destruction. You have been merely dancing all night in the foul air of the ball-room; now you are beginning to spend your mornings in study. You have been incessantly stimulating your emotions with concerts and operas, with French plays, and French novels; now you are exerting your understanding to learn Greek, and solve propositions in Euclid. Beware!! Science pronounces that the woman who studies is lost."

—R.R. Coleman, M.D., Birmingham, Alabama

President Marion Park of Bryn Mawr with Prof. Joseph Breasted of the University of Chicago.

Bryn Mawr Archery team, 1926.

But the *real* radical went beyond what her background predicted. One woman sailed to the South Seas at a time when few women traveled anywhere alone. Margaret Mead became the greatest anthropologist of her time—and one of the greatest authorities on adolescence to this day.

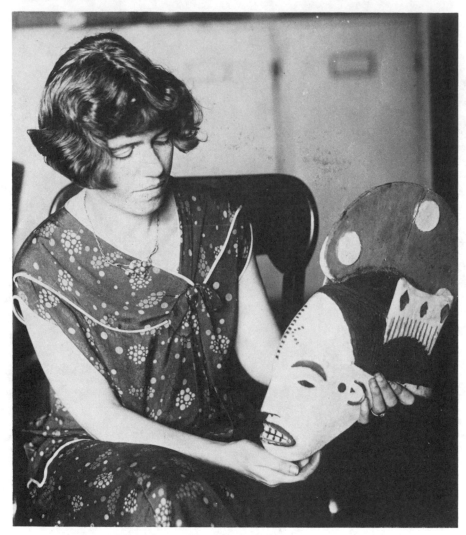

"I had no reason to doubt that brains were suitable for a woman, as I had my father's kind of mind. Which was also his mother's."
—-Margaret Mead

casino de paris

Business had no formula for the future of a black woman. *Her* assembly lines in the 1920s were the fields of the southern farms, and the inside of other people's kitchens. One escape was show business, but that too had its limits.

Josephine Baker's background predicted that she would be limited to clowning around in segregated vaudeville. But she went to Paris with an American company—and she didn't come back.

She took Europe by storm; adopted French as her language; adopted orphans of every color as her own children.

She would speak out against racism before many Americans had even heard the word. But even in self-imposed exile, she longed for home. "I have two loves," she sang. "My country...and Paris." She was the queen of the Folies Bergère.

JOSÉPHINE BAKER

STUD
PIAZ

Back home, what a black woman sang was the blues. Bessie Smith was one of the great blues singers who flourished in an era of speakeasies and easy money, when the hottest night life was up in the clubs of Harlem.

She died in Tennessee as the result of an automobile accident because a nearby white hospital refused to take her in. She was 43.

Bessie Smith's blues lamented the long lonely night of broken hearts.

**My man's got a heart like a rock cast in
   the sea
I hate to see de ev'nin' sun go down—
   Hate to see de eve-nin sun go down.
   Cause my baby he done lef dis town
Feelin' tomorrow lak Ah feel today—
   Feel tomorrow lak Ah feel today.
   I'll pack my trunk—make ma get away.**

—W.C. Handy

But Ida Cox sang a more triumphant lyric. According to her blues, a real woman in love was just like a businessman: she took control of her own time and motion. But in 1929 even the businessmen lost control.

Set your alarm clock, papa;
One hour—that's proper.
Then love me like I like to be.
. . . .
I'm a one-hour mama,
So no one-minute papa
Ain't the kinda man for me.

—"One Hour Mama", sung by Ida Cox

69

DATES FROM THE DECADE

1930

47% of undergraduates are women.

1931

Herbert Hoover signs Act making "The Star-Spangled Banner" the national anthem.

1932

Franklin Delano Roosevelt elected President.

1933

Prohibition repealed.

1935

Largest salary earned is William Randolph Hearst's; second largest is Mae West's.

Social Security Act creates federal-state system of unemployment and old-age compensation.

1936

King Edward VIII of England abdicates out of love for Wallis Warfield Simpson, an American.

1938

Patent issued for nylon.

STAGE

BROA

VARI

Published Weekly at 154 West 46th St., New York N. Y. by
Entered as second-class matter December 22, 1905 at the P

VOL. XCVII. No. 3

NEW YORK, WEDNES

WALL ST. LA

Going Dumb Is Deadly to Hostess
In Her Serious Dance Hall Profesh

A hostess at Roseland has her
problems. The paid steppers consider their work a definite profes-
sion calling for specialized technique
and high-power salesmanship.

DROP IN
ROPES

Honk on Winchell

When the Walter Winchells
moved into 204 West 55th

Many Weep
Christmas
Shows Hit

OWAY

SCREEN

IETY

PRICE 25¢.

ety, Inc. Annual subscription, $10. Single copies, 25 cents
ffice at New York, N. Y., under the act of March 3, 1879.

AY, OCTOBER 30, 1929 88 PAGES

AYS AN EGG

TOCKS
HOWMEN

nd Call Off
ders — Legit

Kidding Kissers in Talkers Burns Up Fans of Screen's Best Lovers

Talker Crashes Olympus

Paris, Oct. 29.
Fox "Follies" and the Fox

Boys who used to whistle an
girls who used to giggle when lov
scenes were flashed on the scree
are in action again. A couple o
years ago they began to take th
love stuff seriously, ... despite

For some people in the Depression, the only way to make money was to dance 90 hours straight and win a dance marathon. The trick was to hang on.

In New York's Riverside Park and all over the country, there were places called "Hoovervilles" where the homeless camped in shanties. They were named for the President of the United States.

By 1933, sixteen million people—*one-third* of the American labor force—were out of work, and the hopes of the nation grew old on the bread of poverty.

In a country that still had segregated everything—including blood banks—the Depression was just about the only thing ever to be separate . . . but truly equal.

Reality was what people starved on. What they lived on was dreams. Hollywood provided the Great Escape.

Like most fantasies she was female, and in all ways a contrast to the real Depression woman. Busby Berkeley's dreamgirls were well fed and robust when many women were thin and weary. They reeked of money; you were as broke as the bank. They made beautiful music; you couldn't even remember when last there was a song in your heart. No wonder women loved *Gold Diggers of '33* every bit as much as men and spent their precious quarters to see them.

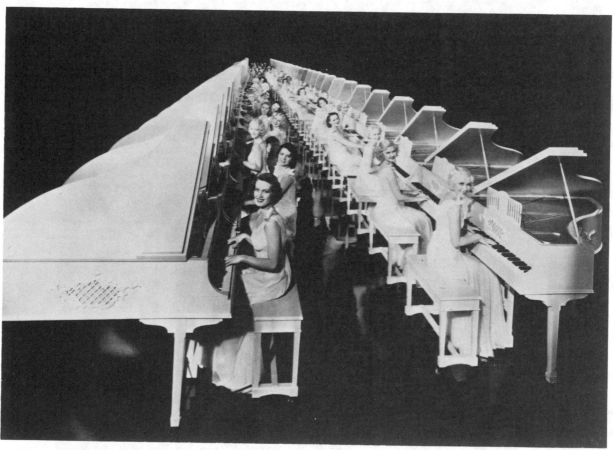

"I saw and approached the hungry and desperate mother, as if drawn by a magnet. I do not remember how I explained my presence or my camera to her, but I do remember she asked me no questions . . . She told me her age, that she was 32. She said that they had been living on frozen vegetables from the surrounding fields and birds that the children killed. She had just sold the tires from her car to buy food. There she sat in that lean-to tent with her children huddled around her and seemed to know that my pictures might help her, and so she helped me. There was a sort of equality about it."

—Dorothea Lange, describing her most famous photograph

The vamp returned in the person of Mae West. She wrote much of her own dialogue in her movies and made the laughs sexier and the sex funnier than ever before. "Goodness what lovely diamonds," said the hat-check girl in *Night After Night*. "Goodness has nothing to do with it," West replied. She laughed off her problems with censors. "It's hard to be funny when you have to be clean," she said. "I used to be Snow White," she philosophized, "... but I drifted."

Innocence came back too, in the person of a new superstar—Shirley Temple. She was healthy and hopeful, and as well fed as Mae West. She even sang about candy, in *Good Ship Lollypop*.

Now that nobody was listening to business any more, the Government of Franklin D. Roosevelt took over the role of advisor...getting housewives on their feet to support the National Recovery Administration...putting the rural poor on their feet with needed social services. Survival was a national priority.

So strength in a woman actually became acceptable. Eleanor Roosevelt may have been shy by nature and reserved by training, but she got her courage from her conscience. She went where no President's wife had ever gone...out of the house of privilege and into the heart of the people.

At self-help exchange, 1937

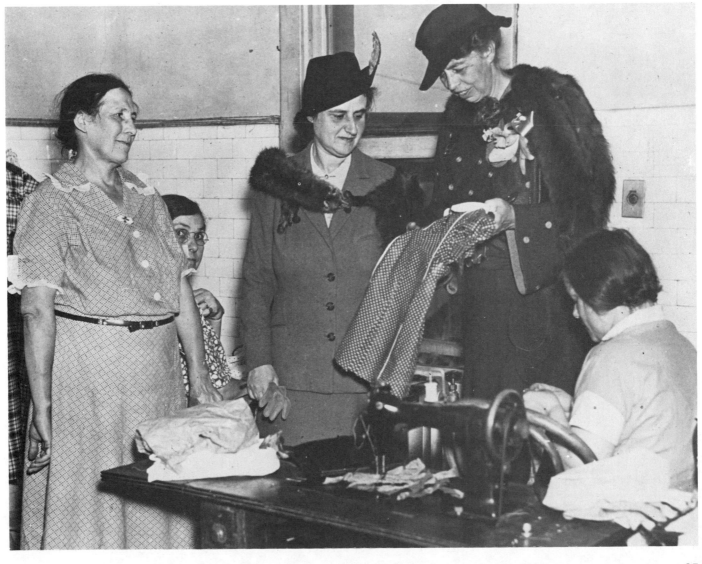

The New Deal brought electrical power to the depressed American farmlands—and that in itself transformed the routine of the farm wife.

Now, she had lights—and some vital new appliances.

For the first time, the country household began to resemble the city household, and women were finally connected . . . by their kitchens.

The new source of advice was the radio, the fourth biggest industry by 1935. To Roosevelt, the radio was a national plat-

"Can an orphan girl from a little mining town in Colorado find happiness as the wife of a wealthy and titled Englishman?"

—Introduction to "Our Gal Sunday"

form for governmental advice and encouragement in the form of "Fireside Chats."

But to the Depression housewife, the radio was the greatest escape of all. Both city and country women shared a new passion in common—the soap opera. The soaps were so sad, they made an American woman's troubles forgettable by contrast. They were called soap operas because, more often than not, they were sponsored by the cleaning companies. And like cleaning, they were assumed to be a woman's medium.

They offered fantasy beyond her wildest dreams.

Radio actors, 1936

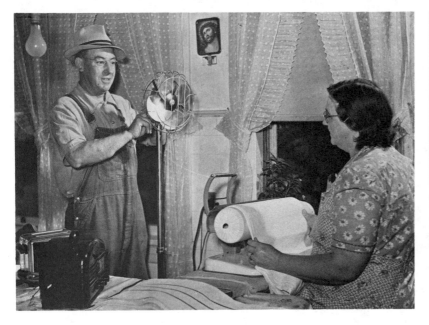

Even the soap ads seemed to be coming from another planet: "Are you always immaculately dainty when your husband comes home from work? Don't let perspiration spoil your attraction for him. Make your home into Heaven. Right before he's due to arrive, whisk off your clothes and take a refreshing deodorizing bath with Palmolive."

At a time when the nation was too poor to be immaculate, the most unromantic of household activities—cleaning—suddenly became the key to romance. And the bad wife was the one who didn't catch every speck of grease and grime. "I could feel his eyes accusing me . . . ," said the wife in the DRANO ad. And she could. And they did.

"you ought to have a Drāno-Day"

what is *your* Drāno-Day?

MON	TUE	WED	THU	FRI	SAT
2	3	4	5	6	7
9	10	11	12	13	14
16	17	18	19	20	21
23	24	25	26	27	28
30					

DISHES TO DO . . . a date to keep . . . and a lazy drain. What a temper-trying combination! She ought to have a Drāno-Day . . . and she *will* have, after this. That's the one day each week on which she'll pour a little Drāno down the drain of every wash-bowl, sink and tub. It's a real time, temper and trouble saver, for regular use of Drāno keeps drains free-flowing *all the time.*

TUNE IN "Hello Peggy," thrilling twice-a-week program on stations WBAL, WBBM, WBEN, WBZ, WCAU, WCCO, WDAF, WFAA, WFLA, WGY, WHAM, WHO, WJR, WLW, WOR, WRC, WTAM, KDKA, KFI, KGO, KJR, KMOX and KOA. Follow Peggy's love-story, the heart-throbs and adventures that go on behind the scenes of a telephone switchboard in a big hotel. See your newspapers for days and time.

Drāno
cleans AND opens drains
REGULAR USE KEEPS THEM FREE-FLOWING

Copr. 1937, The Drackett Company, Cincinnati, Oh

WINDEX *makes window washing easy!*
SIMPLE. No heavy buckets, no messy rags. **EASY.** Just spray on Windex or apply with a cloth. **SPARKLE.** Windows crystal clear—and they stay clear longer. Get a bottle of Windex, today. Made by the makers of **Drāno**

A Lovely Skin Invites Romance!
go on the
CAMAY MILD-SOAP DIET!

This lovely bride, Mrs. R. M. Thorsen, of Evanston, Ill., says: "I've found the Camay Mild-Soap Diet a beauty treatment that really works for new loveliness."

This thrilling beauty idea is based on the advice of skin specialists—praised by charming brides!

HAVE YOU EVER heard a man say of another woman—"Her skin is lovely" —and wondered what he was thinking of yours? Wonder no longer—be sure your skin enchants—invites romance! Go on the Camay Mild-Soap Diet!

Let this exciting beauty treatment bring out all the real, hidden loveliness of your skin. For, without knowing it, you may be cleansing your skin improperly . . . or using a beauty soap that isn't mild enough.

Skin specialists advise a regular cleansing routine with a fine mild soap. And Camay is *provably* milder than dozens of other popular beauty soaps.

Thousands of Camay brides have been helped to loveliness by the Camay Mild-Soap Diet! Follow their example. For at least 30 days use Camay faithfully night and morning. From the first, your skin will feel fresher. And in a few short weeks greater loveliness may be your reward.

CAMAY THE SOAP OF BEAUTIFUL WOMEN
Trade Mark Reg. U. S. Pat. Off.

GO ON THE MILD-SOAP DIET TONIGHT!

Work Camay's milder lather over your skin, paying special attention to the nose, the base of nostrils and chin. Rinse with warm water and follow with thirty seconds of cold splashings.

Then, while you sleep, the tiny pore openings are free to function for natural beauty. In the morning—one more quick session with this milder Camay and your face is ready for make-up.

August 1942 Good Housekeeping

Pottsville, Pa. workers demon-
strate to demand a $15.00 weekly
minimum wage, 1932

As Hard Times eased off, blue collar men and women fought to save themselves from the economic insecurity that had made them such easy victims of the Depression in the first place.

The stakes were high.

The strikes were violent.

And the women were in there, fighting to support the men and the union.

**There once was a
union maid
who never was afraid
of goons and ginks
and company finks
and the deputy sheriff
who made the raid.**

**She went to the
union hall
when a meeting
it was called
and when the
company
boys came round
she always stood
her ground.**

**This union maid
was wise
To the tricks of the
company spies.
She couldn't be fooled
by the company stool.
She'd always organize
the guys.**

—"Union Maid"
by Woody Guthrie

To the women of such an era, a real heroine had to be strong, independent, and exemplify the spirit of survival.

Amelia Earhart was a natural. They called her First Lady of The Air.

She spoke out for women's rights. She and her husband, publisher George Putnam, wrote a marriage contract that promised both of them freedom in work and play.

Dear GP,

There are some things which should be writ. Things we have talked over before—most of them.

You must know again my reluctance to marry, my feeling that I shatter thereby chances in work which means so much to me. . . .

In our life together I shall not hold you to any medieval code of faithfulness to me, nor shall I consider myself bound to you similarly. If we can be honest I think the difficulties which arise may best be avoided.

Please let us not interfere with each other's work or play, nor let the world see our private joys or disagreements. In this connection I may have to keep some place where I can go to be myself now and then, for I cannot guarantee to endure at all times the confinements of even an attractive cage.

I must exact a cruel promise, and that is that you will let me go in a year if we find no happiness together.

I will try to do my best in every way.

A.E.
February 8, 1931

Amelia Earhart

With her husband, publisher
George Putnam

Another heroine of the thirties was Mildred Ella Didrikson Zaharias. They called her "Babe," because as an athlete, she was on par with Babe Ruth. She began as a basketball player, broke Olympic records in track, javelin, broad jump, high jump. Then, twenty years later, she took up golf and became a champion at that too.

The crowds made it clear that strong women were now something to cheer about.

Bette Davis in "Jezebel"

Even Hollywood hired them.

Katherine Hepburn. She was actually taller than Spencer Tracy. She didn't defer to him. She didn't even marry him.

Bette Davis. She had the nerve to play villainesses, to look downright ugly, to sue the studio (she lost, but set an important example in actor revolt).

Davis, Hepburn, and others, like Rosalind Russell, made power in a woman look glamorous. And that was just as well. . . .

Because with men going overseas, the war plants needed women. And *Fortune* magazine said that "woman power" would provide "the margin of victory" in this, the second great war of our century.

Rosalind Russell in
"His Gal Friday"

DATES FROM THE DECADE

1940

Life expectancy rises to 64 years (from 50 in 1900).

1941

Japan attacks Pearl Harbor; Germany and Italy declare war on U.S.

1942

Pacific Coast Japanese-Americans relocated to detention camps; released in 1944.

1945

U.S. drops atomic bombs on Hiroshima and Nagasaki

1946

Emily Greene Balch, founder of Women's International League for Peace and Freedom, wins Nobel Peace Prize.

Winston Churchill delivers his "Iron Curtain" speech at Fulton, Missouri, marking the beginning of the Cold War.

1948

Truman upsets Thomas E. Dewey for President.

Alfred Kinsey's *Sexual Behavior of the Human Male* published.

1949

Ingrid Bergman leaves family for Roberto Rosselini; scandalized fans boycott her films.

This was the way the government tried to inspire sacrifice in American women in a wartime propaganda film called *To The Ladies*. It began with street scenes in a "typical" town:

"'This is Middleton U.S.A., just an average American city like thousands of others. Some of the girls are down at the pool; some are having their afternoon soda down at the corner drug store; others are catching the matinee. Yes, life is pleasant in Middleton; these women are proud of their city.

"This is Middleton, when the women of England and the women of Russia are fighting our enemy with every ounce of blood and muscle in their bodies, when the women of Italy have lost the strength to fight. This is Middleton, U.S.A., in the throes of total war.

"While the women of Middleton perfom their little household tasks, their sons and brothers, their schoolmates and their friends, prepare themselves for their job . . . a job of killing and being killed."

During WWII nearly 265,000 women answered the recruiting call—"Free a Man to Fight."

Women in the Army—100,000
Women in the Navy—90,000
Women in the Marines—19,000
Women in the Coast Guard—11,000

Eighty-three Military nurses were interned as P.O.W.'s on Guam and in the Philippines.

Nearly 2,000 received military decorations for bravery and meritorious service.

The Army and Navy nurse corps reached peak strength. The Army had 51,000 nurses, the Navy had 11,000.

Approximately 1,000 WASPs flew a total of 60 million miles on operation assignments in 77 different types of aircraft.
—Pentagon Office of Women's Affairs records

No effort was spared to get those "ladies" out of their homes and into overalls. William Moulton Marston created "Wonder Woman" as a comic strip character in 1942 to be their inspiration. And they responded. In the war plants, for the first time, some black women got work that paid well. And some black and white women even worked side by side.

Th number of women in the work force rose from 12,500,000 in 1940 to 18,500,000 in 1945.

A grateful country nicknamed her "Rosie the Riveter." And in a propaganda film called *Women of Steel*, a grateful government praised "these mothers, wives, and sweethearts" who "stand shoulder to shoulder with their men . . . these marvelous women of America! . . . those Women of Steel!"

EVERY MINUTE COUNTS

IBM offices

Factory scene

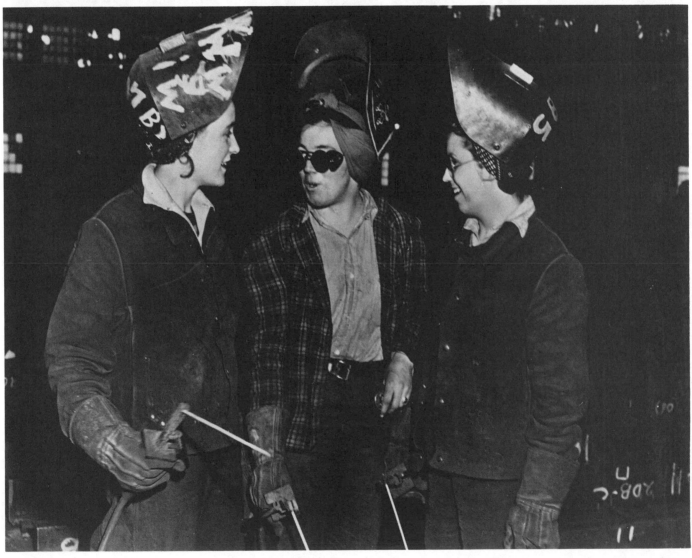

Freight yard worker

Riveter

Sewing parachutes

Welders

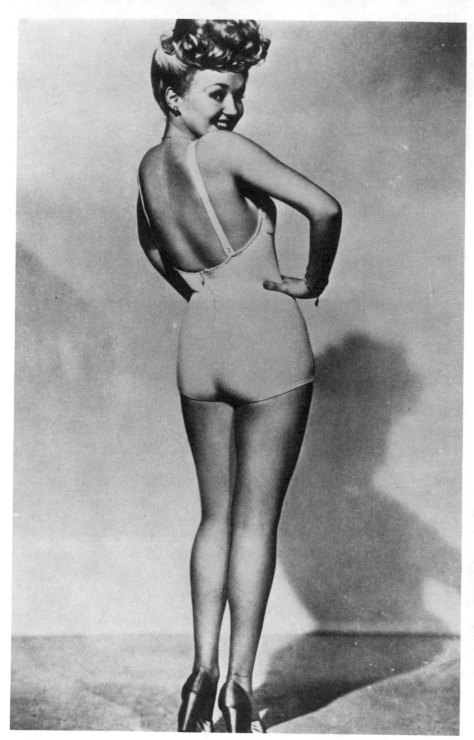

But on the walls of his battleship, his tank, his plane, the GI carried with him through the terrible conflict a very different vision of the girl he wanted to come home to. She was a pin-up; Betty Grable. No overalls. No welder's mask. It was said that the bra Jane Russell wore was designed along the same principle as the nose cone of a guided missile. Power was definitely not the source of their glamour.

The soldier also wanted his old job back. "Last year it was kill the Japs," said Frederick March in *The Best Years of Our Lives*. "This year it's *make money*." So the government made films advising Rosie the Riveter to ignore her skills, doubt her strength, and go back to being somebody's baby:

Betty Grable

V.E. Day, New York, 1945

110

Jane Russell

S ince 1930, one U.S. woman in every four, has been earning her own living," intoned the announcer. "Today, the woman with a position in business equal to a successful man's, is economically able to terminate her marriage if she is so inclined, since she is her own breadwinner. But are such women really better off?"

Many women stayed on in the job market after the war. But the newsreels in the movie theatres warned them they were no longer being patriotic, that they were making a big mistake. One newsreel produced a career woman, Dr. Marynia Farnham, to put down careers for women. Her best-seller, *Modern Woman: The Lost Sex*, invoked Freud to prove that independent women were unnatural, even slightly sick:

"Abandoning their feminine roles has made women unhappy because it has made them frustrated. It has made their children unhappy because they do not have maternal love; and it has made their husbands unhappy because they do not have real women as partners. Instead, their wives become their rivals."
— Dr. Marynia Farnham

The Second World War was the first during which soldiers had been tested for their *psychological* fitness to do battle. And to the horror of the military authorities, thousands and thousands failed the test. Who was to blame for this catastrophe? A new Freudian villainess emerged. Her name was "Mom."

Wives would not be far behind moms. It was awful to think that the puny little man about to be devoured by the monster woman in James Thurber's cartoon was the American soldier coming home from the war.

"Megaloid momworship has got completely out of hand. Our land, subjectively mapped, would have more silver chords and apron strings crisscrossing it than railroads and telephone wires. Mom is everywhere and everything . . . disguised as good old mom, dear old mom, sweet old mom, your loving mom, and so on; she is the bride at every funeral and the corpse at every wedding. Men live for her and die for her . . . and I believe she has now achieved . . . a spot next to the Bible and the Flag . . . ."

—Philip Wylie, *A Generation of Vipers*

One way to deflate
the powerful war-
time woman was to
make her feel bad
about her appear-
ance. An explosion
of advice on love and loveliness
sent American women on a
frantic search for a new look
and a better body. And the new
scientific advisor was her
beautician.

Her reality was reshaped
completely in the fifties.

The bumps were all
smoothed out.

The truth was concealed.

Not since the turn of the
century had there been such a
vast difference between the real
woman and the doll she was
now advised to be.

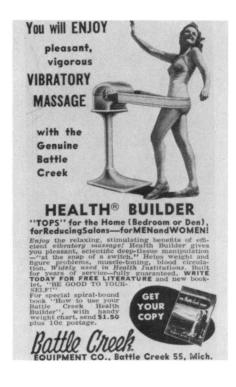

This design is Munsingwear's brief, famous figure-maker (so brief, so firm, it could be the making of a bathing suit). This year? A double-knitting: cotton inside, nylon outside, so that it's cool, fast-drying and shape-retaining (it s *and* yours).

—underwear ad, 1953

DATES FROM THE DECADE

1950

South Korea invaded by North Korean troops; Truman orders U.S. forces into area.

1951

22nd Amendment, limiting the Presidency to two terms, is passed.

1952

Dwight David Eisenhower elected President.

Tuskeegee Institute reports, for the first time in 71 years of compilation, no lynchings in the U.S. that year.

1953

Korean Armistice signed.

Alfred Kinsey's *Sexual Behavior of the Human Female* published; American edition of Simone de Beauvoir's *The Second Sex* published.

1954

Brown v. Board of Education of Topeka: The Supreme Court finds racial segregation in Public Schools "inherently unequal."

1955

Bill Haley's "Rock Around the Clock" becomes first rock n' roll hit.

1957

Soviet Union launches Sputnik I, first man-made satellite.

1959

Alaska and Hawaii admitted to union.

Beauty contestants with their
faces covered so as not to distract
the judges from their legs.

An American girl was supposed to have fun in the fifties. Albert Einstein had declared that, "radio active poisoning all life on earth is now within the range of possibility." But it was men who had to worry about the bills and the bomb and the Cold War with Russia. The girl in the beauty contest appeared oblivious of all that. She smiled; she moved with great care.

"We do this not to *worry* you, but—uh—or frighten you, but really, we gotta admit we live in an atomic age. There *is* an atomic bomb. So we have to be aware of this and know what to do in case an emergency happens."

–Host of 4-H Club TV show for children

In Atlantic City, 1952, Colleen Kay Hutchins of Utah poses with runners-up after becoming Miss America.

Albert Einstein

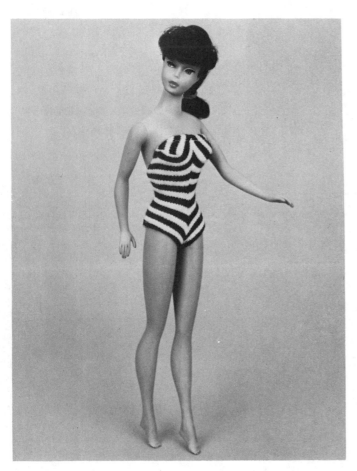

She was built to please. On the big screen, innocence came back into vogue; heroines like Annette Funicello and Sandra Dee were as babyish as they could be and still have breasts. And the Barbie Doll was introduced; she was the ideal woman.

For a man, the only dream going was success. For a woman, the only success was marriage. And in 1950, Liz Taylor was the most beautiful bride of all. By 1951, one out of every three American women was married, like Liz, at nineteen.

Elizabeth Taylor's first wedding,
to Conrad (Nicky) Hilton, Jr.

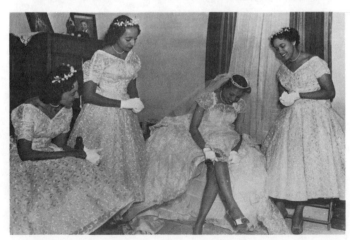

Elizabeth Taylor's fourth wedding,
to Eddie Fisher, Las Vegas, 1959

Long Island Housing Development

Two-thirds of the growth of the American population was occurring in the suburbs, where the government was helping GIs build their dream houses.

His dreamhouse was

her dollhouse. He had to fill it with every major appliance to make them both happy. Mixmasters. Blenders. Clothes dryers. With all these new household toys at her fingertips, she now had no excuse not to be the perfect—and perfectly happy—homemaker.

"H-Bomb Hide-away," 1955

America's favorite housewife was Lucille Ball. Lucy showed that a wife's role was to inspire generosity in her husband any way she could. Once she even pretended it was their anniversary when it wasn't, to see what presents Ricky would bring her.

With the Cold War getting hotter, and bomb shelters in the backyard, fashion tried to recall the safe old days. Crinolines came back for the first time since 1910.

William Frawley, Desi Arnaz, Lucille Ball, Vivian Vance in "I Love Lucy"

One advisor who spoke to women as adults was the famous baby doctor, Benjamin Spock. He said that only women could take care of children, and later regretted it. But in the fifties when everyone thought housewives just had fun, Spock at least understood how much they had to cope with. He was the male authority while her other man was away at work.

And when the man of the house came home, the whole family played with the newest toy: TV. Television became the new source of advice; it showed everyone what family life was supposed to be.

Women were advised by newsreels that in marriage, as in fashion, the old style was safest.

"The family was solidly founded on the father as patriarch and breadwinner, and on the mother as cook, housekeeper, and nurse of the children. Whether marriages were happy or not, people made the best of them, for divorce was almost unthinkable."

—Newsreel narration

Doris Day and James Garner in
The Thrill of It All

Divorces rose by 15 percent between 1958 and 1959. So did sales of major appliances. Clearly a houseful of toys was not enough.

Many Doris Day movies demonstrated how delicately a woman who wanted *more* had to pry open the door of the dollhouse. In *The Thrill of It All* with James Garner, she gently suggested that "the PTA and home-bottled ketchup" were "not very fulfilling" and begged for the chance to work on a TV show just one day a week, promising all the while that she would never neglect her "wifely duties." Garner gave in.

The rebel of the time was the woman who grew up and spoke up. In 1950, Helen Gahagan Douglas ran for the Senate in California against Richard Nixon. "Pipsqueaks like Nixon and McCarthy are trying to get us so frightened of Communism," she said, "that soon we'll be afraid to turn out the lights at night."

Nixon accused Douglas of being "pink right down to her underwear," and he won the election.

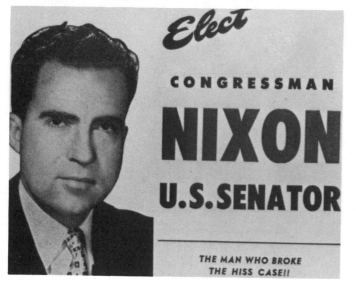

Elect

CONGRESSMAN

NIXON

U.S. SENATOR

THE MAN WHO BROKE
THE HISS CASE!!

America's favorite girl was Marilyn Monroe.

She was our super-doll.

The new vamp, without the old sting.

The whole country had fun with Marilyn...

And she looked like she was having fun too.

She died of an overdose of barbiturates when she was 36.

During the filming of *The Seven Year Itch*, 1955

With Jack Lemmon in *Some Like It Hot*, 1959

With fans on the set of *The Misfits*, 1961

Marilyn Monroe

Few people called things what they were in the fifties. It was an *age* of euphemism. Never mind that girls went crazy for Elvis Presley's gyrations. Ed Sullivan only televised him from the waist up. Never mind that Liz Taylor was marrying for the fourth time by 1959. Marriage was still a dream. Korea wasn't a war. It was a "police action." Women didn't go to the toilet. They went to the "little girls' room," and "powdered their noses" there. Sex was a harmless game. A good girl didn't let her boyfriend get to first base. And absolutely not to second base. Only bad girls went "all the way."

1960

Kennedy defeats Nixon for President.

1961

Bay of Pigs invasion of Cuba fails.

Thalidomide exposed as dangerous drug that deforms fetuses.

First U.S. military companies arrive in Vietnam.

1963

Congress passes Equal Pay Act.

Kennedy assassinated by Lee Harvey Oswald.

1964

Lyndon B. Johnson wins Presidency, beating Barry M. Goldwater by a landslide.

"Beatlemania" sweeps the country.

1966

National Organization for Women founded.

Human Sexual Response by Masters and Johnson published.

Medicare program goes into effect.

1967

Rioting in 127 cities.

1968

Riot at Democratic Convention in Chicago; Hubert Humphrey nominated, Richard M. Nixon elected President.

Feminists picket Miss America Contest.

1969

Armstrong and Aldrin walk on the moon.

500,000 people participate in 4-day rock festival in Woodstock, New York.

But the 1960s made it easier to be a "bad girl" than ever before.

In 1960, doctors found a foolproof way to prevent pregnancy. The Birth Control Pill. The Pill was its own advice. It said, now, you can get everything you want. And singer Janis Joplin tried "everything" else too. She died at **33.**

The pill led to the mystique of the single girl, the most independent woman since Rosie the Riveter. She got advice from *Cosmopolitan* magazine . . . on the pill . . . on men . . . and on orgasm.

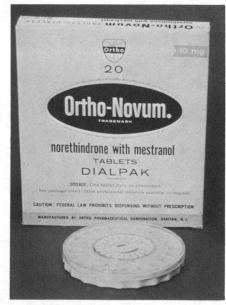

Janis Joplin died
October 3, 1970

But one model single girl never slept with her boyfriend. As "That Girl," Marlo Thomas was the first TV heroine to work for a living and live alone. Housewives, too, had a new model on television: Julia Child. She was the first woman in public memory to be called a "chef." When she messed up, right there on the TV screen, every woman had permission not to be the perfect homemaker.

Marlo Thomas and Ted Bessell in
"That Girl"

"When you flip on these things, you really, you just have to have the courage of your convictions, particularly with a loose mass [of potatoes] like this. No, that didn't go very well. You see when I flipped it, I didn't have the courage to do it the way I should have. You can always pick it up again, and if you're alone in the kitchen, who is going to see?"

—Julia Child

The First Family in Palm Beach, Florida, 1963; Jacqueline, "John John," Caroline and President Kennedy.

If a woman wanted to shed her cares in the sixties, she could become a flower child. If she wanted to show she cared in the sixties, she could join the Peace Corps, a creation of the administration of John Kennedy. His wife, Jackie, urbane and sophisticated, became the new ideal of style. And Kennedy

himself made idealism stylish.

"Let the word go forth from this time and place," he said in his inaugural address, "to friend and foe alike, that the torch has been passed to a new generation of Americans...born in this century, tempered by war, disciplined by a hard and bitter peace, proud of our ancient heritage."

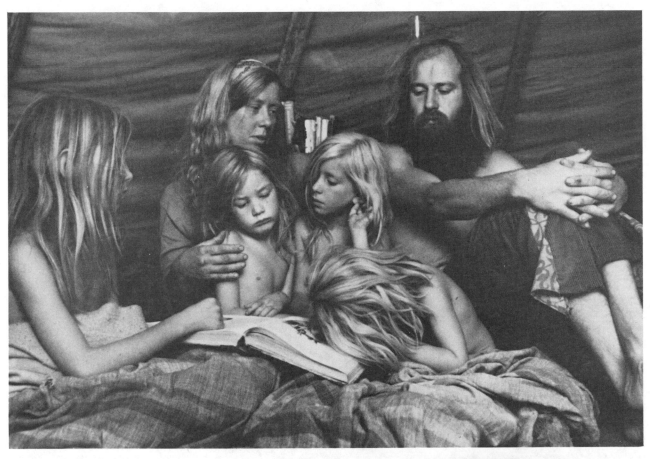

Fannie Lou Hamer

Kennedy's New Frontier program looked at reality and said, with hard work, we could change it for the better. And no one heard him more clearly than black Americans. The heroine of Lorraine Hansbury's *Raisin in the Sun* cried out in her slum apartment:

"I will work and I will slave. I will work my fingers to the bone and wash all the sheets in America! . . . But we gotta get out of here!"

Some men in the civil rights movment belittled the role of women (Stokely Carmichael, for one, described the position of women in SNCC as "prone"). But it was Rosa Parks who had started the revolution. Back in the 50s, she had refused to give up her seat on a bus to a white man. And her subsequent imprisonment had triggered the crusades of Martin Luther King.

It was hard to believe that women were meant to be docile followers of history when a person like Fannie Lou Hamer was emerging as a leader.

"I'm sick and tired of being sick and tired."

—Fannie Lou Hamer

Dr. Martin Luther King, Jr. with Rosa Parks at a dinner given in her honor by the Southern Christian Leadership Conference at a previously segregated hotel, Birmingham, Ala. 1965.

Peace Parade, New York, 1969

No woman could remain unaware of Vietnam, the most televised war in history, and the way it was dividing her country.

Jane Fonda was loved for opposing the war. And hated for it.

"I used to be Barbarella. I had a lot of blond hair and wore falsies and false eyelashes, and I was a movie star. But as far as I knew, all a woman could do was change sheets or something like that."

—Jane Fonda

Jane Fonda as a peace activist, and as "Barbarella"

any men in the peace movement belittled the role of women. "Women made peanut butter," said one New Left activist, "they waited on tables, cleaned up, got laid. That was their role." But it was hard to believe that when you heard Bella Abzug calling for and end to the war and a new beginning. For some a new beginning meant freedom from the revolving door of the welfare system, so the "Poor People" marched on Washington, too.

Some of the marchers were old hands at protest. When she was in Congress, Jeannette Rankin had voted against entry into World War One and World War Two. She had not changed her stand.

"This Mother's Day will commence a mighty women's movement, a movement in every state of this country, in which the women of this country will organize their political power . . . to build a society for our sons, and everybody else's sons, and for people here and across this country."

—Bella Abzug

Woman in "Resurrection City," Washington, D.C., 1968

Jeannette Rankin (center) still
marching for peace, 1968.

Mothers marched against the war.

And for the war.

The images from television made the woman who stayed home think about *her* life. With all the fast foods and gadgetry now available, she still worked fifty-five hours a week, three hours longer than the housewife of the twenties, and then as now, it was the same thing: *nobody thought she was working!*

There was a problem. Betty Friedan's best-selling book, *The Feminine Mystique,* called it the problem "that has no name."

Doctors had no name for it either, but they had a "cure"; they gave her tranquilizers.

But there was no pill strong enough to obliterate her

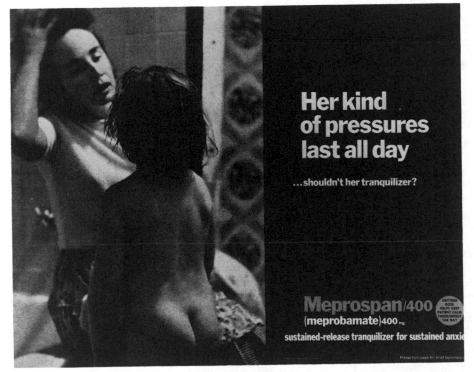

Her kind of pressures last all day

...shouldn't her tranquilizer?

Meprospan/400
(meprobamate)400 mg.

DAYTIME DOSE HELPS KEEP PATIENT CALM THROUGHOUT THE DAY

sustained-release tranquilizer for sustained anxie

Please turn page for brief summary

malaise. One by one, all the treasured sources of advice were being discredited.

Rachel Carson had said in *The Silent Spring* that chemical pesticides would stop "the song of the birds and the leaping of the fish in the stream." Could the scientific advisors have been wrong?

Ralph Nader had declared that the typical American automobile was a rolling death trap. Could the business advisors have been wrong?

In 1970, the government put a label on the birth control pill that said it was associated with heart attack, stroke, damage to the retina...Why hadn't the government known all that before? What else was her doctor wrong about?

Her tranquillity was shattered.

Jackie Kennedy had become a widow . . . by assassination.
Ethel Kennedy had become a widow . . . by assassination.
Coretta King had become a widow . . . by assassination.

Jacqueline Kennedy with her
brother-in-law, Attorney General
Robert Kennedy, at President
John F. Kennedy's funeral, 1963.

Coretta Scott King with her daugher, at Dr. Martin Luther King, Jr.'s funeral, 1968.

Ethel Kennedy with her brother-in-law, Senator Edward Kennedy, at the funeral of Robert Kennedy, 1969.

Two young people died in the demonstrations at Jackson State.

Four young people died at Kent State.

They were somebody's children. And even if they weren't her children, whether she was a housewife or a single girl, whether she was for the war or against the war, at home or marching, white or black, young or old, she could feel the pain. And it changed her.

Jackson State

Kent State

I started having a dream in the 60s," wrote a young reporter named Gloria Steinem. "In the dream I am fighting with someone. They are trying to kill me, or kill someone I love. I'm fighting with all my strength. But I just can't hurt them. They just smile. It must be a classic dream of powerlessness and rage."

DATES FROM THE DECADE

1970
First national women's strike declared on fiftieth anniversary of passage of suffrage.

U.S. population crosses two million mark; national fertility study shows almost zero population growth.

1971
26th Amendment grants voting rights to 18-year-olds.

National Women's Political Caucus founded.

1972
Nixon defeats George McGovern.

Ms. magazine founded.

1973
Supreme Court legalizes abortion.

Watergate. Nixon resigns.

1974
Little League admits girls.

1975
End of Vietnam war.

1976
Jimmy Carter beats Gerald Ford for Presidency.

"Hyde Amendment" cuts off Medicaid funding of abortions.

1978
First "test-tube" baby born.

Congress passes bill extending by three years and three months the timetable for ratification of ERA.

1979
U.S. Embassy personnel taken hostage in Iran; returned in 1981.

Gloria Steinem

In the seventies, that sense of powerlessness gave way to a new sense of strength—in numbers. Women got rid of their old advisors and for the first time, the new ones were mostly women—like Gloria Steinem.

"We have no desire at all to take over the male role. This revolution—and it *is* a revolution, not a reform—is about humanizing both roles, not exchanging them."

—Gloria Steinem

Fifty thousand women march down Fifth Avenue, August 26, 1970 in celebration of the fiftieth anniversary of suffrage.

Thousands marched for the right to choose abortion; after the 1973 Supreme Court decision, thousands marched to keep that right.

Some of the new advisors were women of achievement. It wasn't only what they said but what they *did* that expanded every woman's belief in her own possibilities.

A woman won the Nobel Prize for Medicine—Roslyn Yalow.

A woman ran for President—Shirley Chisholm.

Barbara Walters was the first newswoman to earn a million dollars a year, salary.

Attorney Sarah Weddington won a milestone case before the Supreme Court protecting a woman's right to choose an abortion, and later became a top advisor to the President.

Shirley Chisholm

Rosalyn Yalow

Barbara Walters interviewing Fidel Castro.

In the tennis battle of the sexes, Billie Jean King beat Bobby Riggs, and helped women gain equal pay in sports.

Janet Guthrie was the first woman to race at the Indy 500.

One by one, the achievements added up and influenced what Americans thought a woman could be.

Even Madison Avenue reflected those expanded horizons.

The future President of the United States deserves a nice dry place to grow up in.

And there's no drier diaper than Quilted Pampers.

Pampers

T

his man's Army" became her army too, along with the benefits of job security and training it offered.

A basic trainee of "B" Company
(Fort McClellan, Alabama) gets
comfortable with her new M-60
machine gun, 1976.

A mechanic for the 724th Main
Battalion (Fort Stewart, Georgia)
tunes up the engine of an army
five ton truck.

The army faced the facts of
life and issued a maternity
uniform.

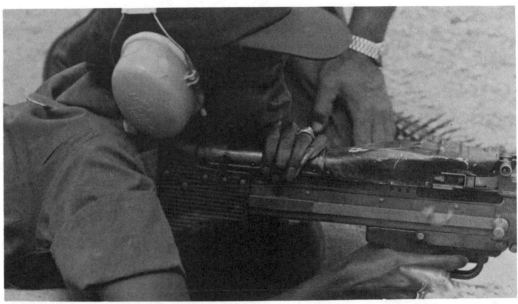

She could be a playwright like Ntozake Shange; a rabbi like Sally Preisand; a Supreme Court justice like Sandra Day O'Connor; a governor like Ella Grasso...a pint-size slugger in the Little League.

Supreme Court Justice, Sandra
Day O'Connor

Ella T. Grasso, Governor of
Connecticut

Theatre poster for Ntozake
Shange's "Colored Girl's"

Rabbi Sally Preisand

187

Last mile of torch relay—Seneca Falls to Houston. Billie Jean King; Susan B. Anthony, grandniece of the suffragist; Bella Abzug; and far right, Betty Friedan.

First Ladies Rosalynn Carter, Betty Ford, and Lady Bird Johnson at Houston Conference.

No matter how different their lives appeared, women were discovering how· much they had in common. At the First National Women's Conference in Houston, 15,000 elected delegates from every state and style of life were joined by three first ladies and heard unusual new advice from Barbara Jordan.

"We know that beauty and brains are not mutually exclusive. We know that we can be as competent in the boardroom as in the bedroom. We *know* that."

—Barbara Jordan

Representative Barbara Jordan of
Texas, keynote speaker in the
Democratic National Convention,
1976.

Washington *Post* publisher, Katharine Graham, withstood threats and backed her paper's exposure of Watergate.

In the fields of California, the farm workers took one of their own to be chief negotiator for them—Dolores Huerta.

Soprano Beverly Sills stepped up from the stage of the New York City Opera and ran the whole show.

And in *Norma Rae,* which was based on the achievements of a real woman named Crystal Lee Jordan, Sally Field stepped up on a table and organized the union.

Dolores Huerta of the United Farm Workers

Sally Field and the real "Norma Rae," Crystal Lee Jordan.

Katharine Graham, publisher of
the Washington *Post*.

Beverly Sills of the New York
City Opera.

The advice of the seventies was "Face the Truth" —and women grew up on it.

Humorist Erma Bombeck wrote what suburban homemakers had always known: *The Grass Is Always Greener Over the Septic Tank*.

Masters and Johnson told the truth about sex—one orgasm was as good as another.

On TV, America's new favorite housewife, Jean Stapleton, played Edith Bunker facing a rapist. That helped erase the myth that rape only happened to women who asked for it.

When First Lady Betty Ford spoke openly of her mastectomy, millions went for breast cancer exams, and lives were saved.

But telling the truth was sometimes dangerous. When Martha Mitchell spoke up about Watergate she was laughed at and left alone.

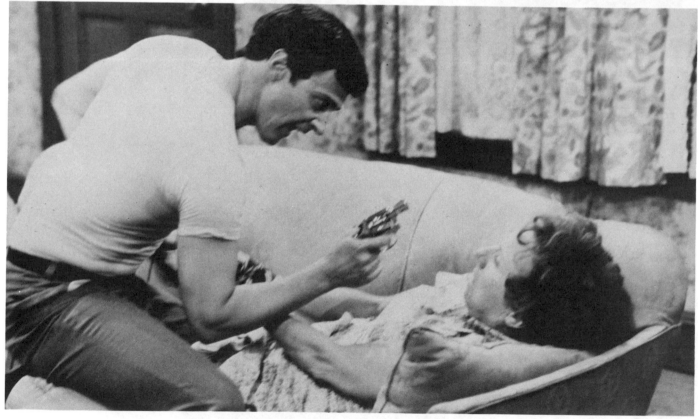

David Dukes and Jean Stapleton in a segment of "All in the Family."

Betty Ford with President Gerald Ford after her mastectomy.

Martha Mitchell, wife of former
U.S. Attorney General John
Mitchell who resigned during the
Watergate scandal.

Sometimes people didn't agree on what the truth was. The proposed Equal Rights Amendment stated simply that "Equality of Rights under the law shall not be denied or abridged by the United States or any state on account of sex." But opponents, like Phyllis Schlafly, mobilized opposition to equality for women even thought the polls showed the majority of Americans continued to support it. And in 1982, the ERA was defeated for lack of ratification by three states.

Still, the real woman had found *her* truth.

She wasn't a flapper anymore, or a paper doll, or a flower child, or anybody's baby. By the turn of the eighties, she was a full-grown, independent woman, and on the *strength* of that, she could face the future.

Phyllis Schlafly

Bella Abzug, Katie Pottinger,
Gloria Steinem, Dick Gregory,
Betty Friedan, Elizabeth
Holtzman, march for the ERA
extension, 1978.

DATES FROM THE DECADE

1980

Reagan defeats Carter.

1981

John W. Hinkley shoots President Reagan.

1982

Time magazine cover story on herpes epidemic.

750,000 people join anti-nuclear rally in New York City.

ERA extension runs out, June 30.

1983

Unemployment passes 11%.

Memorial dedicated to 57,939 who died in Vietnam

Runner Mary Decker Tabb sets three women's distance records.

"M*A*S*H" goes off the air in a blaze of record-breaking-viewer glory.

"Saturday Night Live," the iconoclastic TV humor show hit home with a sketch in which Lily Tomlin (with Dan Aykroyd and Gilda Radner) instructs women hardhats in the fine art of harassing attractive male passersby.

Role reversal got even more complex in *Tootsie*, in which Dustin Hoffman learns how to be a better man after experiencing life as a woman.

Yet another twist to the gender game, *Victor/Victoria*, featured Julie Andrews (with Robert Preston) who manages to find a career *and* marriage playing a woman-disguised-as-a-man-disguised-as-a-woman.

"Hill Street Blues," a gritty police story, features three very different roles for women: Fay Furillo (Barbara Bosson), activist and ex-wife of the station's Captain; Lucy Bates (Betty Thomas), police officer; and Joyce Davenport (Veronica Hamel), attorney and the second Mrs. Furillo, in all but name—she kept her own.

Jennfier Hart (Stephanie Powers) took Jonathan Hart's (Robert Wagner) name in marriage, but is an equal partner in adventure and crisis management. The Harts are a rare TV couple who are happily married and have no children.

On her 65th birthday Lena Horne took her hit one-woman show on tour for a year and told sell-out audiences about her fifty-year career that began in Harlem's Cotton Club and her determination to confront racism.

In her act Bette Midler has broken all the boundaries of "ladylike" behavior. Her outrageous monologue on the Queen of England ("the whitest woman in the whole world") and "mermaid-in-a-wheelchair" numbers are classics. She also played the self-destructive Janis Joplin-like rock singer in *The Rose*.

Twins Paula and Pam McGee
became stars in the newest
women's sport to go pro. Throughout the 1980s new events for women were added to the Olympics.

Weight lifting, a totally new sport
for women, exemplifies the
decade's spotlight on fitness, both
in challenging female physical
limits and allowing competitors to
achieve all-around personal
well-being.

Well-being includes "good sex" ("*with* contraception!") according to straight-talking sex advisor Dr. Ruth Westheimer, whose call-in radio show became a national platform for questions many people didn't know enough to ask a decade earlier.

Many thrived on being accepted into non-traditional career fields from which women had been excluded because of supposed physical inferiority.

Women executives of the 1980s found ways of including comfort and health in the business day.

Lois Gibbs never intended to become a heroine, but in her fight against toxic waste in the Love Canal she became an expert who testified at HEW (Department of Health, Education & Welfare) hearings and an inspiration to other environmental activists.

Yoko Ono, avant-garde artist, musician, breaker of rules, and husband John Lennon shaped a rock idiom whose primary themes were pacifism and concern for humanity. Together they also worked hard to achieve an egalitarian marriage and shared parenting. In 1980 John was assassinated, and now Yoko sings alone.

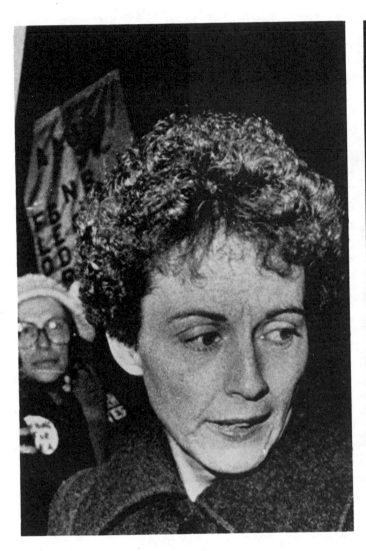

A lifelong dedicated Mormon, Sonia Johnson wrestled with her God and emerged determined to defy church doctrine and support the Equal Rights Amendment. She was excommunicated, but continued to fight.

In the spring of 1983, Sally Ride "liberated" the most exclusive male club in America and became the first American woman astronaut (and flight engineer) in outer space.

Jewel Jackson McCabe, political activist and media executive in New York City, built on the emerging power base of black women professionals and executives to form the "National Coalition of One-Hundred Black Women" to celebrate and exercise that power.

Jane Byrne won the race for mayor of Chicago, one of the most politically baroque cities in the country.

204

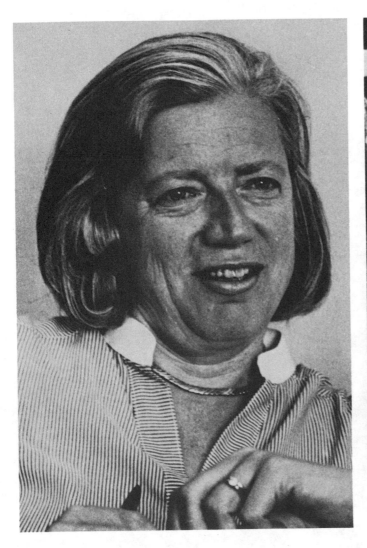

Hanna Gray was appointed the first woman President of the University of Chicago amid predictable controversy, but managed to concentrate on the giant institution's academic and financial problems.

In 1983, Alice Walker became the first black woman to win a Pulitzer Prize for fiction (for her fourth novel—*The Color Purple*). She has been producing daring and textured work about the South for more than a decade.

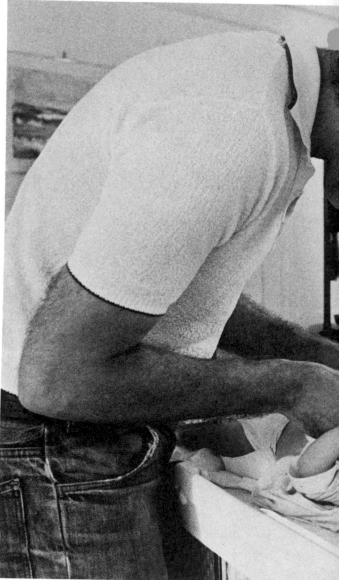

As opportunity for women expanded, so did research on the female body. It turned out that pregnancy is not a disease and that parenthood does not have to be a stay-at-home occupation. Track star Debbie Brill exemplified both truths: she set a world record less than three months after giving birth to her son, who is often at the stadium when his mother competes.

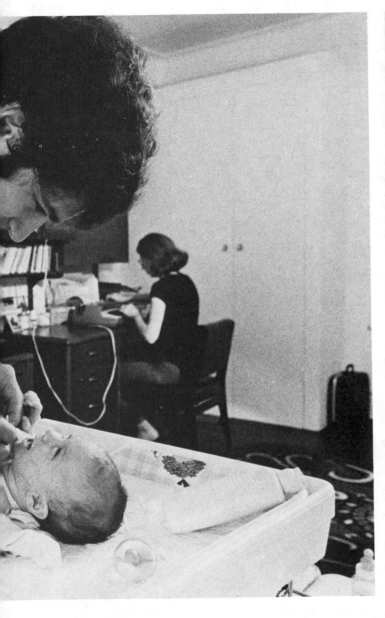

As for the stay-at-home part of child rearing, a very simple principle emerged: the parent who can, does.

And their daughters would make the world in their own image.

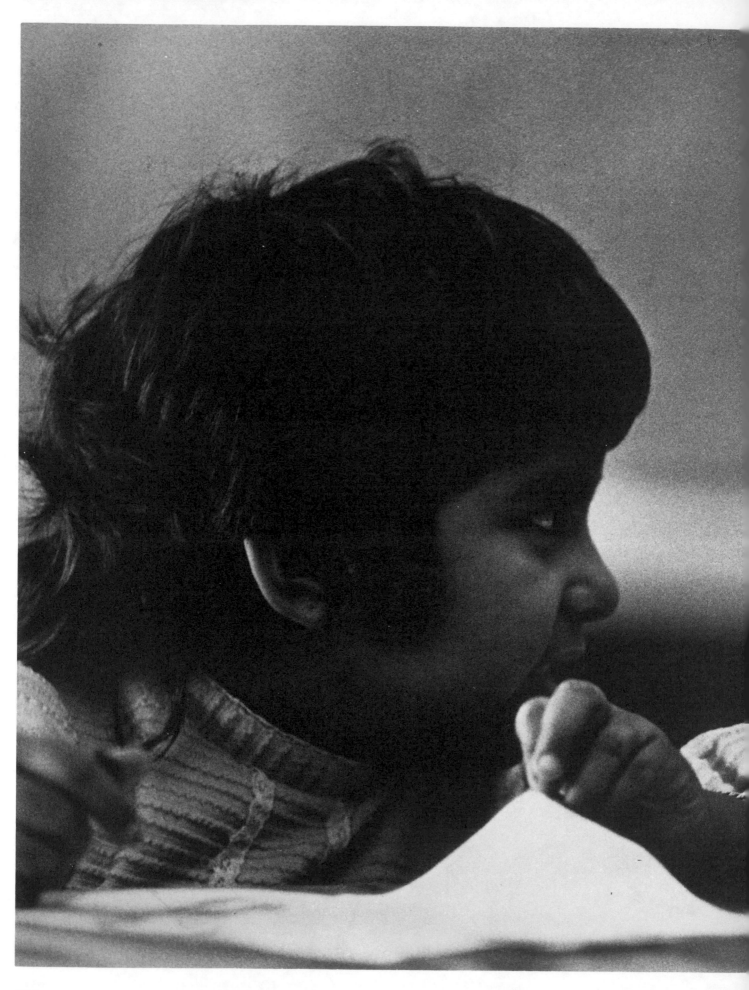

FILM CREDITS

PRODUCTION CREDITS

Executive Producer
Suzanne Braun Levine

Producer/Director
Ana Carrigan

Writer
Susan Dworkin

Editor
Mili Bonsignori

Associate Producers
Liesel Friedrich
Karin Lippert

Assistant Editor
Elizabeth Shore

Music Consultant
Ethel Huber

Stills Filming
Michael J. Davis

RESEARCH

Film
Nan Allendorfer
Mary Lance

Stills
Sheree Crute

Text
Annette Fuentes
Della Rowland

Historical Consultants
Barbara Ehrenreich
Alice Kessler Harris

*This film is available for
sale or rent from;
MTI Teleprograms, Inc.,
3710 Commercial Avenue,
Northbrook, Illinois 60062
(800) 323-5343.*

PHOTO CREDITS

Credits should be read from the left to the right of each spread.

INDEX

Page numbers in *italics* refer to illustrations.